FRANKLY FRANCHISING

DEMYSTIFYING FRANCHISING TO HELP YOU INVEST IN THE BEST FRANCHISE FOR YOU

PAM BARTLETT

Printed in the United States of America

Published in Hellertown, PA

Cover design by Jennifer Giandomenico

For more information or to place bulk orders, contact the author or the publisher at Jennifer@BrightCommunications.net.

Bright

COMMUNICATIONS

CONTENTS

FOREWORD

In today's ever-evolving business landscape, where opportunities abound and entrepreneurial spirits soar, the decision to buy a franchise holds tremendous potential for aspiring business owners. Franchising offers the unique advantage of combining the autonomy of business ownership with the support of a proven system and established brand. However, navigating the intricacies of the franchise buying process requires careful consideration, strategic planning, and expert guidance.

As a franchise lawyer with extensive experience in assisting individuals on their journey to franchising and franchise ownership, I am honored to introduce this comprehensive guide on buying a franchise. Within these pages, you will find a wealth of knowledge, practical insights, and invaluable advice that will empower you to navigate the complex world of franchising with confidence and clarity.

Franchise opportunities vary widely, spanning industries as diverse as pet care services to full-scale restaurants. Each franchise possesses its own unique set of requirements, demands, and rewards. By truly knowing yourself, your strengths, and your aspirations, you will be better equipped to identify the franchise opportunity that aligns with your goals and suits your personal and professional inclinations.

In choosing a franchise, it is crucial to recognize the value of seeking professional guidance. Franchise consultants play an indispensable role in this process, offering their expertise, industry insights, and comprehensive support. These experienced professionals possess a deep understanding of the franchising landscape and can guide you through every stage of the buying process. From evaluating franchise options to conducting due diligence and negotiating terms, their knowledge and resources will prove invaluable as you make informed decisions on your franchise journey.

I have had the privilege of witnessing the transformative impact of franchising in the lives of countless individuals. From the fulfillment of lifelong dreams to the realization of financial independence, the franchise model has the power to unlock a world of possibilities. By immersing yourself in the insights shared within this book and engaging the services of trusted consultants, you will be equipped with the tools necessary to embark on this exciting path with confidence and clarity.

The past few years have seen franchising grow by leaps and bounds, and I predict that trend will continue. Certainly, the franchise model is here to stay. In the United States, we have tremendous demand for excellent goods, services, and businesses, and that's what franchising does. It helps to spread successful goods, services—and businesses.

I'm pleased to welcome to you the wonderful world of franchising. May you find it as fascinating, fruitful, and fun as I have!

—Mike Drumm, Esq.

Founder, Drumm Law, Denver, Colorado

www.drummlaw.com

MY FRANCHISE JOURNEY

Back in 2013, I was downsized from Corporate America for the third time. It was a strange time for me; I was 55 years old, and recently divorced. In a way, that also meant I was unencumbered—free to discover what the right next move for *me* was. At the same time, I was concerned that at my age it would be difficult to find a job, plus I didn't want to risk going through yet another corporate restructure, only to find myself back in the same position. Maybe you stand at the same type of crossroads!

Over the years, many people had told me that I should own my own business, but I never wanted that responsibility. I liked being an employee. Unfortunately, I reached a point in my life where I was feeling like my destiny had not been in my own hands, and I thought I should at least consider that as an option. *At least I'm not going to down-size myself!*

I decided if I was going to own my own business, I should explore all my options. I really had no idea what I wanted to do, and I no vision of what *my* business would be. I knew nothing about franchising, but thought I should at least look into it and see if it made sense. Like most people, I thought of franchising as McDonald's and Subway, but those types of business did not interest me.

Because I didn't know anything about franchising, I started

researching it. I discovered there are people whose work is to help other people invest in franchises. That sounded like exactly what I needed—someone who could fast-track my understanding!

In my Googling, I had found a few franchise consultants, and I set up a meeting with the first one who called me back.

I talked with that consultant for about an hour. At the time, I was disappointed that he didn't seem terribly interested in getting to know me, and he didn't even take the time to get to know my skillset. He basically took my financial information, glanced at my resume, then presented me with franchise options.

I had absolutely no interest in three of them. But the fourth, senior care, piqued my interest. Both of my in-laws had been dealing with dementia, and I had recently lost both of my parents. The opportunity to help other people navigate those rough waters appealed to me.

The more I learned about investing in a franchise, the more convinced I became that I had enough experience to be able to run a business. Plus, I knew that investing in my own franchise would allow me to earn a good living. Most importantly, I believed that investing in a franchise would give me greater control of my success.

And it did! I bought that senior care franchise, and I ran it for nine years.

There were many things I loved about owning a franchise:

- I was in control of my own destiny.
- I had more control over my own finances than I did as an employee.
- I loved having the support of a corporate entity, but I was "the boss." Other than following the (proven) system, I didn't answer to anyone.
- I loved having peer support that you don't get when you're in business by yourself.
- When the Covid-19 pandemic hit, my franchisor stepped in with legal advice and was able to get us the personal protective equipment that was so scarce in the beginning. (We were an essential business in the healthcare world.) My

"independent" counterparts in the industry struggled with these things.

On the other hand, there were some things I didn't love about owning a senior care franchise:

- I thought I did my due diligence, but I was unprepared for the day-to-day level of stress of a senior care business. (It's life and death, 24/7.)
- I didn't love the senior care industry. I think my consultant mostly looked at which franchises I could afford—not really recommending franchises that I would enjoy.

After nine years running my senior care franchise, I was ready to do something different, and I wanted to get away from owning a 24/7 business. In a bit of serendipity, one of my neighboring franchisees wanted to buy my territories. It was the perfect time to think about selling.

I had hired a general manager to run the day-to-day operations of my franchise so I could take a step back. Because I wasn't devoting all of my time to running my franchise anymore, I had the time to look for something else to do. At that point, I had no idea what that was.

I didn't want to invest in another franchise at this point in my life—though I considered it. Little did I know the best next step for me was still within the franchise world.

I didn't have to look too far for my next opportunity. One day, I received an email from a gentleman who was starting a new franchise consulting company, and he was recruiting franchise consultants to join his team. Even though I had worked with a consultant to buy my senior care franchise, I didn't know what franchise consultants did. I replied to his email, asking to learn more.

We talked by phone, and after I hung up, I thought, *Wow! This is for me!* It felt like it was meant to be. Becoming a franchise consultant would give me the uniquely rewarding experience of guiding people down the path I had taken, enjoyed, and on which I found success.

I decided that this is what I wanted to do, but first I wanted to vet the person who was starting the new company. I told my franchisor I was considering becoming a franchise consultant. I felt it was important that I was transparent with them, since I still owned the business, and I asked if anyone knew the business owner. The person in my franchise who works with consultants gave me some great information and recommended I work with one of the bigger, more established broker networks instead, such as the International Franchise Professionals Group (IFPG).

I thoroughly researched several networks and decided to join IFPG. That was the right decision. It's a great company, the resources are phenomenal, and they have been named Entrepreneur Magazine's #1 franchise consulting network for the past four years.

Once I made the decision to join IFPG, the next step was to go through their intensive training program and become certified.

The more I learned about becoming a franchise consultant, the more I realized I would be happier on that side of the franchise consultant desk! Having learned so much about franchising, from being in the trenches for nine years, I realized I could use my experience and expertise to help people just starting out in the franchise world. I also realized that most people don't understand what franchising is all about. They immediately think of McDonald's and Chik-fil-A. Yes, those are both franchises, but they represent a tiny percentage of the franchised businesses in the US. IFPG represents more than 600 franchises in over 30 different industries. There are many different business models and paths to ownership.

I had served for six years on my franchise's Owner's Advisory Council, so I got to see the business of franchising from both sides. I got a greater understanding of the relationship between the franchisee and the franchisor, and I learned what to look for in a franchise, and what would be red flags.

Owning a franchise is different than being an employee, and that's an adjustment. Having been both, I can guide my clients through the process, and I can also help them know what to expect as they make the transition to business ownership. My experience gave me the insight into what it takes to successfully own a franchise.

So that I can even better help my prospective franchisee clients, I became a mentor with SCORE, an organization that provides free business mentoring. I want to give back. I love helping people, and mentoring with SCORE is similar to franchise consulting.

I love everything about being a franchise consultant. I love working with people who want to change their lives—and helping them do that.

On the flip side, I also love researching franchisors and learning all about them. There are so many great ones.

I've found that the franchise community is supportive and passionate. I'm grateful to be a part of it, and I love helping other people learn more about it as well.

WHAT IS A FRANCHISE?

A franchise is the opportunity to be in business *for* yourself—but not *by* yourself!

A franchise is a tested and proven business system where a franchisee pays an initial fee and/or royalties for the right to do business under a franchisor's name and use the franchisor's systems. It's a unique, interdependent relationship.

A franchise is a lifestyle, and most likely, a lifestyle change. When you invest in a franchise, you are not buying a job. You are investing in your future, and often creating a salable and willable asset. In this book, we don't talk about *buying* a franchise, we talk about *investing* in a franchise. Often you are investing your hard-earned money in your new business and can expect a good return on that investment. While no franchisor can or will promise how much money you will make with your business, the goal is that your franchise will generate a profit, create income, and afford you and your family a comfortable lifestyle. The return you see on your investment is dependent on **you**, and how you run **your** business.

WHY INVEST IN A FRANCHISE?

Have you ever thought about starting your own business, but didn't have an idea what you wanted to do? Without a great idea, the thought of starting a business is overwhelming. Where do you start? Have you considered investing in a franchise?

- Investing in a franchise is an **investment in yourself**, in *your* future. Bank on yourself!
- When you invest in a franchise, you join a brain trust, a network, a community of people willing and eager to support you, collaborate with you, and share ideas and information with you.
- You're investing in a proven system—key to your success— rather than creating it yourself through trial and error.
- You gain access to the franchisor's brand, history, and body of work—rather than spending years creating your own independently.
- The franchisor's system, team, and brand will help you **accelerate your success**!

Frankly Franchising Fact: 10.5 percent of all businesses are franchises, according to the US Census Bureau.

WHY NOT JUST START A BUSINESS?

You might wonder, why shouldn't you just start your own business? Consider:

- The Bureau of Labor Statistics reports that about 20 percent of independent businesses close after two years. Investing in a franchise of an established business gives you a strong foundation upon which to build.
- If you need to finance the purchase, financing the purchase of an existing business can be easier than raising money for a startup.
- It can take years to build a successful business, with no immediate revenue. With a franchise, you can hit the ground running and selling, with only a few weeks of training.

ADVANTAGES OF STARTING YOUR OWN BUSINESS

- The business is all yours. No one will tell you what to do (other than industry/state regulations, if applicable), so you are in complete control.
- There are no limits (again, other than industry and state regulations).

- You will not pay any franchise fees nor royalties.

DISADVANTAGES OF STARTING YOUR OWN BUSINESS

- Having no limits means you must think of *everything!*
- The reality: It is all yours. You are on your own for all aspects of the business, and will need to know everything about marketing, operations, finances, HR, and industry / state regulations.
- The odds for success of a startup business are not great. Slightly less than half will fail within 5 years.

WHY NOT BUY AN EXISTING INDEPENDENT BUSINESS?

Rather than investing in a franchise or starting a company from scratch, what if you bought an independent, existing business—a middle ground?

ADVANTAGES OF BUYING A RESALE BUSINESS

- This option comes with slightly lower risk than starting from scratch because the business has been established. (But be sure to do your due diligence.)
- The business should already have customers and be producing cash flow.

DISADVANTAGES OF BUYING A RESALE BUSINESS

- You do not always get the whole story. There could be two sets of books, and you might not be getting the real value.
- When the owner leaves, the customers might leave too, having been more loyal to the owner than to the business.

ADVANTAGES OF INVESTING IN A FRANCHISE

- You receive training and ongoing support from the franchisor.
- The business already has branding and brand recognition. You might have to establish the brand in your market, but the franchisor will have the materials to help create a strong brand.
- You will have the supportive relationship of other franchisees in your system. Most franchise systems are collaborative environments.
- You will have the advantage of systems and processes that are developed, tested, and even improved over time by the franchisor. Some franchisors will help streamline your operations, which means the backend operations are all handled by the franchisor, such as invoicing, collections, etc.
- Due to the franchisor's level of experience, they can and often will guide their franchisees on how to streamline operations and cut needless expenses.
- Some franchisors help you find leads. For example, they might have call centers that filter leads to their franchisees.
- Some franchisors centralize billing and payroll operations at their corporate headquarters, leaving you to focus on your business growth.
- Your chance of success is much higher investing in a franchise than with an independent startup business.
- When you decide to retire or exit from your franchise, there is often already a strategy in place.

DISADVANTAGES OF INVESTING IN A FRANCHISE

- You need to go through an extensive vetting, interview-type process.
- Franchises are awarded—not sold. The franchisor will carefully consider if you're the right fit to be a franchisee.

- You will need to pay an initial, nonrefundable franchise fee —which can range from $20,000 to more than $60,000 with an average of $40,000.
- You'll receive and review an extensive document called a Franchise Disclosure Document and sign a Franchise Agreement, and you are obligated to follow the franchisors requirements that are spelled out in those documents.
- To set up your franchise, you might need to invest in real estate or rent property, purchase or lease equipment, and hire and train a team.
- You will be expected to follow a system (that has been proven successful).
- Over the life of your business, you will pay your franchisor a royalty and possibly fees, such as a marketing and technology fee.
- You will be held accountable by the franchisor. You must adhere to the franchisor's system standards to ensure the consistent quality of the brand across all markets.
- You might have restrictions on when and where to purchase supplies.
- The franchise agreement is for a set period of time (often 5 to 10 years), after which you need to renew (and generally pay half of the initial franchise fee).

Frankly Franchising Fact: There are nearly 674,000 franchise owners, according to Zippia.

WHAT'S THE DIFFERENCE BETWEEN ESTABLISHED AND EMERGING BRANDS?

When you begin to explore franchises, your consultant will show you a variety of options. Some of those brands might be well-established, with more than 100 franchisees and have been in business for several years. You might also be shown start-up, or emerging brands. Emerging brands are in their early stages of development and may have as few as one franchise, or you could even be their first franchisee. There are advantages and disadvantages to both types of businesses. Let's explore the differences between the two.

ADVANTAGES OF ESTABLISHED BRANDS

- The kinks might have been worked out of the system, and the operations run smoothly.
- There will be a larger network of peers available for you to collaborate.
- There might be a high level of brand recognition.
- There could be a higher level of national ad support.

DISADVANTAGES OF ESTABLISHED BRANDS

- You probably won't have much input into how the business is run.
- The territory you want might already be taken.
- Fees may be higher due to the proven success and strength of the brand.

ADVANTAGES OF EMERGING BRANDS

- You might have more influence over the development of the brand.
- As the brand grows, you can grow with them.
- There will be more desirable territories available.
- You will most likely have more access to the brand's leadership team.
- It's exciting to be part of a new opportunity and be first-to-market!

DISADVANTAGES OF AN EMERGING BRANDS

- The brand will have had less time to prove their success.
- The support team will probably be smaller than an established brand's.
- The systems are less established.
- It might be more difficult to access capital to finance your company.

How do you determine which is best for you? It depends on what you want/need in your franchised business. A franchise consultant can help you work through the best decision for you.

WHAT MAKES A GOOD FRANCHISEE?

Not everyone is cut out to own a franchise. The reason franchises are so successful is because the people who originally created the business created a tried-and-true system that works. It's important to the success of the franchise system that the individual owners follow that system and follow the branding and operational guidelines. If you are someone who cannot follow a system, franchising is not for you. A good franchisee is coachable and willing to learn and adapt to new ideas.

This doesn't mean there isn't room to be entrepreneurial. Another trait of a good franchisee is an entrepreneurial spirit. Putting your own special touches on your franchise can make the difference between a good business and a great one—within the operational guidelines set by the franchisor.

Other attributes that will help with the success of a franchisee is a basic business knowledge. Understanding the Key Performance Indicators (KPIs) of your specific business and managing your business to them will help ensure your success.

Also, understanding how to manage your cash flow is very important. If you come into your business without this basic knowledge, consider working with an organization like SCORE, where you can get *free* one-on-one business mentoring. Many franchisors will also help their franchisees understand the basics of running their specific business, and some even include it in their onboarding training.

Remember, when you invest in a franchise it is *your* business. You are the face of your business in your community. (Or, if you choose to own a semi-absentee business, your general manager is the face of your business.) Good franchisees create goodwill for their brand within their communities.

WHAT'S A CERTIFIED FRANCHISE CONSULTANT?

Franchise consultants, sometimes called franchise brokers, are similar to real estate brokers. Franchise consultants provide consultation services to prospective franchisees—for free. Instead of charging you, the potential franchisee, consultants are paid by the franchisor when a prospective franchisee signs a contract and pays a franchise fee.

You could say a franchise consultant is a professional matchmaker —connecting hopeful entrepreneurs with franchise opportunities. Franchise consultants are like Match.com for franchises.

Franchise consultants can become certified franchise consultants (CFCs) by organizations such as the International Franchise Professionals Group (IFPG). Visit www.ifpg.org to learn more. I've been a CFC since 2021.

CFCs have been through extensive and ongoing training. They follow a code of ethics that protects their franchise candidates, and, as part of a broker network, they have access to hundreds of different franchise opportunities in more than 30 different industries. Consultants aren't given access to a broker's resources without the proper training and certification.

From a candidate's perspective, the franchise consultant definition is a trusted advisor, counselor, educator, and guide. I became a franchise consultant because franchising can be confusing to most people. A CFC will demystify franchising and ensure you understand exactly what is expected.

I think that I offer a lot to my clients because of my background as a franchisee, my extensive corporate background, and my strengths as a leader, mentor, and coach.

My experience as a franchisee, combined with my history of consultative sales, has given me great insight into what it takes to help people find the best opportunity for them—without pressuring and selling. I love working with people, the feeling I get when they tell me how much I've helped them, and how valuable the insights I've shared are to them.

Here's how my process works:

- I meet a prospective franchisee—like you!
- I send you a confidential questionnaire to fill out.
- We talk by phone or zoom so I can learn more about you, including your employment history, financial status, and business and personal goals.
- I tell you more about franchising, and we discuss how it might fit into your plans.
- I research franchise opportunities on your behalf based on what I've learned in our discussions.
- I share some franchise opportunities with you and why I think those opportunities meet your goals.
- If you are interested in any of them, I schedule a call with their team.
- You will have several conversations with them, such as with their development officer, training officer, and founder.
- If they approve you and you approve them, they will send you their franchise disclosure document (FDD) to review.
- You will likely talk with them to ask questions and begin your due diligence, which I will guide you through.
- If you choose to move forward, after a 14-day waiting period, you can sign their franchise agreement, send in your

nonrefundable initial franchise fee and invest in yourself and a franchise!

- Periodically, I'll follow up with you to find out about your experience with the brand.

Frankly Franchising Fact: 92 percent of franchisees were still going strong after two years, according to FranNet.

WHY WORK WITH A CERTIFIED FRANCHISE CONSULTANT?

When you buy a house, you work with a Realtor because they know the available homes, understand what red flags to look for, understand the current market, and know the best financing options. It's similar with a franchise consultant.

CFCs are often compared to Realtors because we perform similar functions with the sea of available franchising options—there are several thousand different franchises across many different industries.

Another benefit is that CFCs spend time getting to know our clients before we begin researching appropriate options to present and get to know our clients' personal and professional goals.

CFCs also have tools at our disposal that the average consumer does not, such as databases, webinars, one-on-one interviews with franchisors, feedback on franchisors from past clients, and a broker network.

What is a broker network? Broker networks consist of two parts, consultants and franchisors. (They also may have a vendor network as part of the brokerage that would include attorneys, financial consultants, marketing companies, and more.) The broker network creates an online data base with detailed information about each of the franchises in its network, which is readily available to consultants. Franchisors know that consultants that are part of a network are given extensive training and will vet their candidates before introducing them to the franchisor. This saves the franchisor time so they don't have to filter through unqualified candidates.

CFCs have been through hours of training to learn the ins and outs of franchising. We also must do ongoing training to maintain our certification.

CFCs take the information we have learned from our clients when we begin our research. We use multiple methods to determine the best options based on our client's goals and stay with them throughout the entire process and advise along the way.

Like our real estate counterparts, CFCs know how to recognize red flags and what is standard in franchising. We have access to vetted franchise attorneys, accountants, and other resources to help guide our clients to an informed decision. CFCs have a fiduciary responsibility to our clients, and we act in the best interests of the client. We do not charge our clients for our services, and instead we are paid a referral fee by the franchisor for a successful placement.

Frankly Franchising Fact: Franchises account for about 3 percent of our national GDP.

HOW DO I FIND THE BEST FRANCHISE?

This is a question consultants get asked all the time. The simple answer is: The best franchise is the one that is right for *you*!

As a certified franchise consultant, my job is to understand your experience, interests, goals, and needs—both emotional and financial. I'll help you to learn:

- Do the financials for a particular franchise meet your needs and fall fit within your budget?
- What does a typical day in the life of a franchisee look like?
- How does the franchisor define their ideal candidate?

These are just a few of the things to consider when you are vetting a franchise. It would be my pleasure to help guide you through the process to finding—and investing in—your best franchise!

WHAT TYPES OF FRANCHISES ARE THERE?

If you're reading this, you've decided to explore franchising, and the myriad of opportunities. Just about any type of business you can think of can be—and has been—franchised. Franchises are an important element in the US economy. There are more than 750,000 franchise locations in the US, employing more than 8 million people, and accounting for more than $800 billion in sales. I predict that number is going to continue to grow.

We're experiencing a tremendous change in the way we work. In 2020 during the pandemic, working from home became not only the norm, but a necessity. The pandemic changed the way Americans work. One of the biggest shifts was that companies learned that their workers could be productive without being in the office.

Then in 2021, more than 47 million Americans quit their jobs. In 2022, we were talking about the great resignation. In 2023, it's quiet quitting and massive tech layoffs.

These trends are indicative of the fact that people are getting frustrated with corporate America and making money for "other people." What happens to the people who are in their prime working years, but want to leave corporate America? Some might be independently wealthy, but the majority of us still have to earn a living.

Do you want to have more control over your work destiny? Maybe even work from home? Are you looking for a part-time gig or a side hustle? Buying a franchise is a viable option to consider.

There are many ways to own a franchised business, and there are many types of franchises. To guide you in deciding, here are some questions to consider:

- Do you want to go all-in and be a hands-on owner involved in the day-to-day operations, or are you interested in a semi-passive investment where you can keep your day job and work part-time?
- Do you want to work from home or go to an office every day?
- Do you have a passion for a specific industry or are you open to options that you may not have thought of?

Your certified franchise consultant will spend time with you to determine what makes the most sense for you. Here are some things to consider—and talk with your consultant about.

INVESTMENT LEVELS

There are many diverse levels of investment in franchising. When looking at a franchise, it is important to know the "all-in" cost. There is the franchise fee, plus additional startup costs. Your consultant will make sure you understand all these costs before you decide to invest in a business. Start-up costs are in item #7 of the Franchise Disclosure Document. This will show you a low and high range of initial costs.

FINANCING YOUR FRANCHISE INVESTMENT

Do you need help funding your new business? My funding resources can help you to better understand your options and even refer you to third-party lenders who understand and deal with franchise funding each and every day.

Your consultant can introduce you to vetted resources to help you fund your business and find the best strategy for you.

You can tap into several types of lending programs such as:

- Small Business Administration Loans
- Funding from private lending institutions
- Tapping into your retirement plans WITHOUT any fees for early withdrawal
- Using your non-IRA investments as collateral for funding
- Taking advantage of equipment leasing programs that can reduce your overall start-up costs
- Unsecured lines of credit

Choosing the right lending program for your new business will play a big part in your initial and ongoing success, so I am here to help. I can help you understand your options and connect you with qualified lenders, who can help you design the right program for your new business.

WHAT IS THE PROCESS?

If you are considering fulfilling your dream of self-employment, then you've come to the right place. As a member of the International Franchise Professionals Group (IFPG), I know how important this step is to you and your family, and I'm here to help you with your search for the perfect business.

How can I help you? Like all lasting and successful businesses, I have a well-defined process in place. The IFPG process will save you time and aggravation and streamline your search. When you work with me, I'll get you in front of the right franchises and the decision makers at the franchise companies who can answer your questions and provide you with the information you need to make a smart decision.

THE IFPG 4-STEP MATCHING PROCESS

Step 1. Information Gathering

Most ventures–business or personal–are more successful when the right questions are asked *before* they are launched. During your Information Gathering stage, you'll discuss your goals, funding options, previous experience, and personal and business preferences. Everyone is different, and you owe it to yourself to talk to someone who has been professionally trained to ask questions and then actually listen to your answers.

Step 2. Researching Your Options

After we've discussed what you'd like to accomplish and what you have to work with, I'll begin researching and speaking with franchisors on your behalf. As a trained franchise professional, I have resources, tools, and experience that will help streamline the process. My goal is to find four or five franchises that might be the right fit for you.

Step 3. Discussing Your Potential Future Business

Most of my clients really enjoy this step. During this step, you'll hear about the franchises that might be a good fit for you. You'll spend time with me discussing the attributes of these franchise models and why I think that you should consider them. We'll revisit your goals and discuss how these franchises have the potential to meet them.

Step 4. Speaking with Your Future Franchise Partner–The Franchisor

Once we have identified the franchises that you're excited about and feel are potentially a good fit for you, we'll set up a time for you to speak with them directly. This too is an exciting step in the process because you'll be hearing about these franchisors' business models, the daily activities of their franchisees, what it takes to get started, and what it takes to grow your new business.

I'm proud to give you the help and the resources you need to make informed decisions throughout the process. And best of all, my work will never add a single penny to your new franchise investment. Yes, my consultations are completely free, and I'll never ask you to pay me anything!

FRANCHISING YOUR BUSINESS

TURNING YOUR SUCCESSFUL BUSINESS INTO A FRANCHISE SYSTEM

You took the risk and started a business on your own. Congratulations!

One of the best ways to grow your business is through franchising.

The decision to franchise your business is not to be taken lightly, but it can be one of the most rewarding steps you take as an entrepreneur. Franchising is more than just replicating your business model. You're building a community of like-minded people who share your passion and vision.

WHY FRANCHISE YOUR BUSINESS?

You've already learned the basics of franchising, and now it's time to explore why you might consider franchising your business.

Franchising can be exciting and profitable—if it's done correctly. There's no one-size-fits-all approach, and what works for one business may not work for another. It's essential to consider whether your business is ready to franchise. It's also imporant to understand your personal and business goals before you take the plunge.

One of the primary reasons business owners choose to franchise their business is to accelerate their business's growth. Franchising can help you expand your brand's presence more quickly than traditional methods.

Franchising allows a business to rapidly expand into multiple markets and locations—simultaneously. Each new franchised location or unit allows a brand to grow faster than if it added and opened company locations one at a time.

Because most franchise owners are locally based, they will often have a deep understanding of their local market, culture, and consumer preferences. This local knowledge is valuable for a franchise to thrive in diverse markets. However, this can be a challenge to a more centralized type of organization. Franchisees are motivated to effectively market and promote their business in their local areas, and they can tailor their campaigns to their specific market.

Franchising your business also reduces your risk. Franchisees invest their own capital, and they are financially responsible for their day-to-day operations. The risk is distributed between the franchisor and franchisee, lowering the exposure for the franchisor. The franchisee has "skin in the game." Franchisees have made a financial investment, and they are motivated to maintain high standards for the success of the brand.

Franchising can also provide an additional source of capital for your business—without adding debt or giving up any equity. In addition to an initial franchise fee, you will collect royalty payments from all your franchisee's gross sales.

Franchising allows you to scale your business by expanding into new markets and territories without the expense of additional real estate, personnel, and other expenses of opening new locations.

IS YOUR BUSINESS READY TO FRANCHISE?

Do you have a successful business? Do you want to grow through franchising? There are a few criteria you need to meet.

- First, proof of concept. Your business needs to be well established and operating successfully. It is important that your business is profitable and that a franchisee can earn an acceptable living as well as a return on their investment. The concept needs to be able to be replicated. Can you train your franchisees to run their business and replicate yours?

- Does your business concept meet a need or solve a problem? Do you serve a niche market? Identify what makes your business unique, and uncover reasons why this would be attractive to potential franchisees.
- Do you have an identifiable brand? Ensure you have created your brand identity. Confirm that it is consistent across all your marketing materials, including logos and signage.
- Is your business stable? Your business needs to be financially stable and able to provide the necessary support for your franchisees. This might include marketing support, initial and ongoing training, pre-opening support, and other potential assistance your franchisees might require.

WHAT HAPPENS NEXT?

If you are ready to franchise your business, you'll need to take several steps.

I highly recommend that you work with an organization skilled in setting up franchise systems. Franchising is regulated by the Federal Trade Commission, and you will want to ensure that you are legally compliant with all regulations and that you understand the different state requirements.

Your franchise consultant can help you identify the best organization to work with for this process based on the specifics of your business and your needs. Many companies offer franchising services, but not all are equal. They should be thoroughly vetted. Your consultant will help you find the best partner for your specific needs.

The franchise development company should work with an experienced legal team on the following to ensure you are legally compliant with local and national regulations:

- Franchise Disclosure Document (FDD): This legally required document contains important information about your franchise system. This document is crucial for your potential franchisees to understand exactly what to expect from you and what you expect from them. The FDD contains details about your business model, your fees and royalties, territory rights, start-up costs, and much more. It is important that this document is well thought out and appropriately covers your needs as the franchisor.

- Franchise Agreement: This document details the terms and conditions of the franchise relationship.
- Trademark registration: Your attorney should register your trademarks and protect your brand identity.

Additionally, the development company should help you develop an operations manual, which will cover everything your franchisees will need to know to run their day-to-day business successfully and to your standards. This covers all procedures and customer service standards.

The development company will also help you with financial planning. They will work closely with you to help you determine your initial franchise fee, royalty structure, and any additional fees you might need to charge, such as tech fees, marketing funds, etc. They will help you create a financial model that will outline how those fees and royalties contribute to your revenue, and they will ensure you cover your costs for training and supporting your franchisees.

The development company will help you create your support infrastructure to ensure your franchisees' success.

Some franchise development companies will also help you find your franchisees. This can be very beneficial to getting your franchise up and running.

In conclusion: Franchising is not just a business decision. It's a journey, a partnership, and a commitment to the growth and success of your brand.

FRANCHISOR CASE STUDY
BRIGHT COMMUNICATIONS FRANCHISING

THE FIRST BOOK PUBLISHING FRANCHISE!

Do you love helping people? Working with words and books?

Become a Bright Communications franchisee and be in business *for* yourself—not *by* yourself! Here are the top 5 reasons to become a Bright Communications franchisee:

1. Join one of the lowest-start-up-cost franchises.
2. Use your experience and expertise to help other people realize their publishing dreams.
3. Focus on finding authors, editing books, and managing projects—while we support you with invoicing, training, and our efficient, effective process.
4. Work with our team of trained editorial and design professionals—no need to find, hire, and train any employees yourself.
5. Run your business from your home—or anywhere you love.

Our franchise-driven, independent publishing model will revolutionize the publishing industry.

"I worked for 25 years building my business—throwing a lot of spaghetti at the wall to see what sticks, crying, and cursing. If someone had asked me 25 years ago if I wanted to spend 25 years figuring out my business by myself *or* if I wanted to invest $39,900 to buy a franchise, I would have drained my bank accounts, maxed out my credit card, and sold a kidney to buy that franchise.

"I wonder how much more successful I would be today if I had bought a franchise 25 years ago—with a proven program, trained team, franchisor support, and established brand. My franchisees will stand on my shoulders—and I'm taller than I look!"

—Jennifer Bright, founding CEO, Bright Communications

Bright COMMUNICATIONS
Franchising

Why reinvent the printing press?!
Help people bring their books to life!

Path to Ownership

Jennifer Bright	Pam Bartlett	Jennifer Schriffert	Jennifer Goldsmith
Founding CEO	Sales Director	Franchisee Support Director	Training Director

1 Introductory Zoom with Sales Director Pam Bartlett
Review questionnaire, brand history, industry information,

2 Coaching Call with Training Director Jennifer Goldsmith
Review the Myers-Briggs Type Indicator, training process

WEEKS 1-2

3 Opportunity Discovery Zoom with Founding CEO Jennifer Bright
Company information, vision for growth, receive Franchise Disclosure Document (FDD)

4 Franchise Disclosure Document (FDD) Review and Q&A with Jennifer Bright
Review FDD, answer your questions

WEEKS 3-4

5 Meet Our Team
Get acquainted, answer questions

6 Franchise Agreement Delivery with Pam Bartlett and Jennifer Bright
Franchise agreements delivered and signed, fees transferred

WEEKS 5-6

7 Welcome Call with Jennifer Bright
Celebrate! Begin your Bright Communication Adventure! Talk about next steps!

FREQUENTLY ASKED QUESTIONS

There may be no free lunch in life, but The IFPG Free Consultation will never cost you anything, adds great value to your search, and will give you the information that you need to control your franchise search, and by extension, your future. We often hear the following questions about our Free Consultations.

IS IT REALLY FREE?

Yes, it's free. We work with hundreds of Franchisors, Licensing and Business Opportunities and even existing businesses for sale. These businesses use our services to help find qualified and educated buyers. Just as employers pay headhunters or employee placements agencies for finding them the right candidates, these companies pay us directly for helping them find the right franchisees. While our services can be invaluable, you'll never pay anything to us, or anything additional for taking advantage of our free consultation.

DOESN'T USING YOUR SERVICES ADD SOMETHING TO MY START-UP EXPENSES?

No, never. The Franchisors, Licensing and Business Opportunities that we work with understand that when we introduce a client to them, they've been educated about their offering. In short, they use our services to find qualified candidates who understand their business model and who have a strong understanding of their own skills.

WHAT IF I DON'T WANT TO INVEST IN A FRANCHISE OR A BUSINESS? AM I OBLIGATED TO KEEP WORKING WITH YOU?

Of course not. If at any time, and for any reason, you realize that you aren't ready to pursue your dream, simply tell us and we'll wish you luck. Not everyone should own their own business, so if you–or we– discover that you may be better suited doing something else, the process can stop or simply be put on hold.

WHY CAN'T I SIMPLY CONTACT THE FRANCHISES THAT I ALREADY KNOW I LIKE MYSELF?

You can, but you may eventually find out (often after many hours of research and waiting for information) that the Franchises that you like may not be able to meet your goals. That is why receiving help from a trained professional can streamline your search. We have direct access to hundreds of opportunities that understand and appreciate that we help our clients become better educated about business ownership. In short, we can save you time and energy while getting you in front of the right people.

HOW LONG WILL THE FREE CONSULTATION TAKE?

Everyone is a little different, but in general the initial call can take under an hour or in some cases may take two hours. In any case, there is never a fee and when completed, you will have a better under-standing of what contributes to a successful business venture.

THE FINE PRINT

BY MIKE DRUMM, ESQ.

Buying a franchise is a long-term commitment that can occupy a large part of your life (up to 20 years or more!). Just like you would never buy an expensive home without an appraisal or third-party inspection, you should not invest in a franchise without the help of a franchise lawyer.

Here are the top five reasons why you should hire a franchise lawyer before buying a franchise.

1. The franchise disclosure document (FDD) and franchise agreement (FA) are more than 200 pages. Do you really want to read 200+ pages of legal documents? Really? (*See* What a Franchisee Prospect Needs To Know About an FDD)
2. Franchise agreements are like leases. You are making a multiyear commitment. You can't "get out" if you no longer want to operate the business (or the building) without selling (subleasing) or buying your way out. A franchise lawyer will let you know what you are committing to.
3. Franchise agreements in general do not favor franchisees. You already have one strike against you. Let a franchise lawyer make sure your specific franchise agreement does not have a strike two and three as well.

4. Franchise lawyers know where the bodies are buried (i.e. they know what to look for in an FDD and Franchise Agreement). Do you know what is supposed to be in a franchise agreement and what is not? A franchise lawyer does.
5. Franchise lawyers know what is negotiable and what is not.

Looking for a list of questions to ask the franchisor or other resources? Visit our site: https://drummlaw.com/buy-a-franchise.

ABOUT THE AUTHOR

Pam Bartlett is a Certified Franchise Consultant with more than 30 years of business experience working with nationally branded consumer products companies in senior level sales and marketing roles. Though successful, what she desired was the freedom and flexibility of owning her own business. The thought of starting something from scratch was overwhelming, so she decided that the expertise and support of a franchise may be the best option for her. She reached out to a franchise consultant who took time to get to know her, her financial needs, experiences (both life and work), and her short- and long-term goals.

As a franchisee, Pam spent six years on the franchise's Owners' Advisory Council. This gave her an inside look at the franchisee/franchisor relationship. From this experience she decided she wanted to become a bigger part of the franchising industry and share her expertise, so she went through extensive training and credentialing to become a Certified Franchise Consultant.

For more information:

- Email pbartlett@franstrategies.com
- Cell 610-730-2887
- Visit https://franstrategies.com
- Book an appointment: https://calendly.com/franstrategies

ABOUT FRANSTRATEGIES

FranStrategies Franchise Consulting works with people in career transition exploring the possibilities of business ownership. We work with our clients to match them with opportunities that fit their goals, lifestyle, and their applicable skills. We do continuous education on franchises, and help our clients navigate the process so they can make an educated and informed decision.

FranStrategies is a member of the International Franchise Professionals Group (IFPG) and will bring a host of resources to assist you in your search. When you work with a professionally trained franchise consultant you are tapping into a franchise professional who has a process in place to help you succeed in your search for the right business.

HOW WE CAN HELP YOU

- We'll spend the time needed with you to understand what your goals are. Imagine buying a home or even a car without first stepping back to decide what you need and what your investment range should be. You owe it to yourself and your family to start your search with some guidelines in place– that is where we can help.

- After we understand what your personal and professional goals are, we will begin contacting franchisors on your behalf. You will never have to visit websites, request information and then wait around to see if a franchise is potentially the right fit–we will do all of that for you.
- We will show you franchises that you'd probably never even consider on your own. Yes, that is something that an experienced franchise professional, with a deeper understanding of the opportunities in today's marketplace, will regularly do for their clients. If you love coffee, you will probably gravitate to looking at coffee franchises, even though owning a coffee franchise has very little to do with loving coffee. You owe it to yourself to understand what franchise models best align with your existing skills and we will help get that picture into focus.
- If you need financing, we can refer you to 3rd party lenders who specialize in financing franchises. All too often someone's life's dream of franchise ownership is squashed by their local bank's loan officer who many have little or no experience in lending to potential franchisees.

There are many more benefits and services that we can bring to your search, so please visit us at https://franstrategies.com/contact-us to get started.

www.ingramcontent.com/pod-product-compliance
Lightning Source LLC
Chambersburg PA
CBHW071444210326
41597CB00020B/3933